Developmental Coordination Disorder

of related interest

Helping Children with Dyspraxia
Maureen Boon
ISBN 1 85302 881 9

Asperger's Syndrome
A Guide for Parents and Professionals
Tony Attwood
ISBN 1 85302 577 1

Helping Children to Build Self-Esteem
A Photocopiable Activities Book
Deborah Plummer
ISBN 1 85302 927 0

Small Steps Forward
Games and Activities for Pre-School Children with Special Needs
Sarah Newman
ISBN 1 85302 643 3

Developmental Coordination Disorder
Hints and Tips for the Activities of Daily Living

Morven F. Ball

Jessica Kingsley Publishers
London and Philadelphia

First published in the United Kingdom in 2002
by Jessica Kingsley Publishers Ltd
116 Pentonville Road
London N1 9JB, England
and
325 Chestnut Street
Philadelphia, PA 19106, USA

www.jkp.com

Library of Congress Cataloging in Publication Data
A CIP catalog record for this book is available from the Library of Congress

British Library Cataloguing in Publication Data
A CIP catalogue record for this book is available from the British Library

ISBN 1 84310 090 8

Printed and Bound in Great Britain by
Athenaeum Press, Gateshead, Tyne and Wear

Contents

Acknowledgements

Chapter 13, ' When Behaviour is a Problem', was prepared by Lyndal Franklin and Diane Collis, Occupational Therapy Department, Mater Children's Hospital, South Brisbane, Australia. Their superb handout was adapted for this publication.

Thanks to Annabelle Tilbrook (née Nommensen) who co-wrote Chapter 11, 'Organisation', when we worked together in 1995. Annabelle now lives and works as a Paediatric Occupational Therapist in Southern Australia

Grateful thanks to Carol Grant (Voluntary Action, Inverness) for word processing the manuscript and Roddy Robertson for his IT assistance

Thank you to the Highland Developmental Coordination Disorders (HDCD) group for their support and encouragement in pursuing this publication. Thank you to Emma Fraser, pupil at Glenurquhart High School, for designing the HDCD logo which has been adapted for use on the front cover.

Thanks to all the children and families that I have worked with for all their inspiration.

Thanks also go to ex-colleagues who have taught me all the invaluable paediatric OT skills and knowledge I have gained.

Lastly, but not least, thanks to my husband Roger for his patience and thoughts.

CHAPTER I

Introduction

These hints and tips are written for parents and carers of children diagnosed with Developmental Coordination Disorder (DCD). DCD includes dyspraxia, and other associated disorders, such as Asperger Syndrome, Dyslexia and Attention Deficit Hyperactivity Disorder (ADHD). There is a lot of overlap amongst these disorders and many such children will have problems with their social skills, motor-planning, attention and concentration, and coordination. Developmental Coordination Disorder is the name given to the condition where children have difficulty with movement and with specific aspects of learning, and where these difficulties are not due to any other known medical condition.

It is estimated that up to 1 in 10 children is affected by DCD. Therefore, every class teacher and many families will have a child with this disorder, from mild to severe, making it a relatively common condition. There is no magic 'cure', though the child may improve in some areas with growing maturity and with access to the appropriate therapy to develop skills. However, some children respond more completely to treatment than others.

Even when a child is receiving therapy intervention, and support for learning at school, there are often a number of problems for parents and carers to overcome that require practical solutions. These include things such as behaving with socially appropriate skills, learning new tasks and coping with day-to-day demands at home and school. This guide gives very general and simple ideas to refer to on a daily basis to help with activities of daily living (ADLs). It is hoped that the hints and tips will help improve or develop a child's skills. Sometimes little changes can make huge differences in the child's physical skills and behaviour. It is obviously still a very good idea to treat the underlying problems (e.g. low muscle tone, poor balance, poor eye movements) rather than focus solely on functional problems, unless the child and/or yourself feel this is a priority (e.g. tying shoelaces or cutting food). What I mean by this is if the child finds the functional activity physically very difficult then he or she may be reluctant to participate in the task which in turn could lead to increased anxiety and frustration. In these cases tackling the underlying physical problem becomes a priority.

It is essential that the advice of a paediatric occupational therapist be sought. A GP, school doctor, or a paediatrician can refer the child to a paediatric OT working in your local child health service or employed by your local education authority. In some areas an educational psychologist, speech and language therapist, a teacher or even a parent could refer a child. Paediatric OT's are thin on the ground, so the child may have to be referred to another district or seek treatment privately – The National Association of Paediatric Occup- ational Therapists hold a register of private practitioners (see Helpful Addresses). Once a paediatric OT has been found a treatment programme that involves gross motor activities to help increase the child's sensory-integrative function can be drawn up and implemented. Working on gross motor activities often leads to improvements in academic and functional tasks.

In my experience many carers of children with DCD, including dyspraxia and allied conditions, often feel poorly equipped to deal with these children's daily needs. I hope to provide you with enough suggestions to select what is useful for your child. A lot of the ideas are common sense, but you may or may not have thought of these ideas yourself. If you have devised solutions of your own which help your child this is absolutely great. Please share them with others that have a child or work with a child with DCD.

When reading this book and following the tips, please remember that each DCD child is unique, with his or her own set of difficulties. Please bear these points in mind:

- **Allow extra time**
- **Do lots of practice**
- **Praise successes**
- **Use repetition**
- **Do not pressure**
- **Allow variability**

CHAPTER 2

Developmental Coordination Disorder Explained

What is DCD?

Developmental Coordination Disorder is an impairment, immaturity or disorganisation of movement. Associated with this there may be problems with language, eye movements, perception, thought, specific learning difficulty, personality and behaviour, and variability.

Other names

The term DCD is now replacing 'clumsy child syndrome' and 'motor-learning difficulties', often referred to as dyspraxia. In the past various terms have also been used, e.g. sensory-integrative dysfunction, perceptuo-motor dysfunction, minimal brain dysfunction, spatial problems, visuo-motor difficulties. They are all terms for children who have difficulty with movement and with specific aspects of learning.

How does DCD affect a child?

Movement

Gross and fine motor skills are immature and the child finds them hard to learn, making him or her awkward in performance. This may affect balance.

Language

Articulation may be immature or even unintelligible in early years. Language may be impaired or late to develop.

Eye movements

There may be difficulty with controlling movements of the eyes when following a moving object or difficulty looking quickly and effectively from object to object. This may affect eye–hand coordination.

Perception

There is poor registration and interpretation of the messages that the senses convey and difficulty in translating those messages into appropriate actions.

Thought

The child may have normal intelligence, but have great difficulty in planning and organising thoughts. Those with moderate learning difficulties may have these problems to a greater extent.

Specific learning difficulty

There may be problems with reading, writing, spelling, reversals (e.g. formation of numbers/letters) or reversing the order of letters in words and/or numbers, and with number work/maths (e.g. concepts and rote-learning, like times tables).

Personality and behaviour

The child may display behaviour problems, e.g. restlessness, lacking controls, unhappiness, loneliness, poor self-esteem, lack of confidence and/or behaviour problems due to frustration. Secondary emotional problems may develop (e.g. refusing to go to school, bedwetting, difficulty with friendships, becoming easily upset), often caused by pressures on the child from other children and adults.

Variability

Children have 'good days' – when they can do things better than at other times – and 'bad days'. It is crucial to remember this when working with a child with DCD, especially as the child's performance can vary from hour-to-hour.

CHAPTER 3

Posture

Posture is very important for many ADLs, e.g. for feeding, writing, games, schoolwork, homework and so on. Not only is it important for physical control of the body, but it can increase attention and help increase control of eye movements. So – check the child's posture!

Poor posture may be caused by a multitude of things, but most commonly in children with DCD it is due to low muscle tone (lacking normal tone or tension in the muscles so the child feels 'floppy'), resulting in reduced joint stability. Holding a correct fixed position is therefore extremely difficult for them, leading to slouching, restlessness/fidgeting and/or fatigue. Often children have persisting baby-hood reflexes (i.e. primitive reflexes that have not been superseded by more skilled movements and balance reactions) and if sitting posture is not corrected, head movements can affect stability and posture also. Reduced attention span can also make sitting difficult, so sit in a chair at a desk or table rather than sitting on the floor.

17

Tips for achieving good posture

- Good posture is achieved by sitting with the pelvis at the back of the seat with hips, knees and ankles at 90 degrees with feet on the floor or on a foot block (see Figures 3.1 and 3.2).

- The upper arms should never be less than 30 degrees from the trunk.

- A Dycem mat™ (a non-slip sticky mat that does not adhere to materials) on the seat or a ramped/wedge cushion can also be useful (see Figure 3.2).

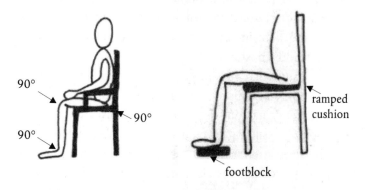

Figure 3.1   *Figure 3.2*

- Stability can be increased with chair armrests/footrests.

- The desk height should be about 2 inches above the level of the elbows when the elbows are bent and the child is sitting upright in the chair.

- Table height is important. Check if the table needs to be raised. A cut-out table (a table with a semi-circle cut out – see Figure 3.3) is great because the child's trunk can fit into the gap and the elbows are supported by the sides, giving stability to the trunk and arms and aiding a more upright posture. These specialised tables can be bought from Rifton or G & S Smirthwaite (see Resources) or a table could be adapted.

Figure 3.3 Cut-out table

- Beware of plastic classroom chairs – the backs tilt and the seats are too long. This results in compensatory postures that limit stability and movement of the arms and hands.

- If you help the child to fix his or her head position looking directly in front, then this will help the child fix his or her eyes in space.

- A slanted desktop or angled surface on the tabletop may help many children avoid a lot of head movement and will help inhibit any baby-hood reflexes that result in altered posture. They are useful if the child loses his or her place easily when reading due to poor relocating.

- When sitting on the floor a cross-legged position is best. This gives more stability than long-sitting or side-sitting, which is more tiring and requires the child to use his or her hands for support.

CHAPTER 4

Writing

There may be numerous reasons why writing is a problem (e.g. the child cannot use his or her hands in isolation from the upper limbs) and this needs assessment from a paediatric occupational therapist. Problems can be caused by:

- low muscle tone

- instability in joints in upper limbs

- persisting baby-hood reflexes

- type of pencil grasp used

- tremor or controlling movement in upper limb joints, i.e. slight arm incoordination.

Poor writing is often caused by fast-fatigue of the muscles within the hand. (Fast-fatigue is the quick development of tiredness and pain in the muscles – most individuals do not experience writer's cramp unless they have written for a lengthy period.) Sometimes the children grip a pencil with more force because they do not get good proprioceptive and/or tactile feedback. If the child has dyspraxic problems then layout and organisation can be poor.

Common problems and how to minimise them

Grasping the writing implement

Holding a pencil can be a very difficult task for a child with DCD. The child may not feel the pencil in his or her hand adequately due to poor tactile sensation, so he or she may not be able to adjust their grasp, know how tightly or loosely they are holding the pencil or know how hard they are pressing. Poor proprioception can also cause an ineffective grasp, excessive joint movement and poor detection of force.

- With low muscle tone you tend to grip tighter to get a strong grasp, so increasing shaft size reduces gripping/grasping pressure.

- Use an elastic band at the bottom of the pencil to prevent the fingers slipping down the pencil (see Figure 4.1). Put the elastic band about 1inch from the tip.

Figure 4.1 Elastic band

- Use a pencil grip (see Figure 4.2) or a triangular pencil. These are available from HOPE, GALT and Nottingham Rehab (see Resources).

- Paint a ring round the pencil to indicate where it should be held.

- Colour code places on the pencil and the child's fingers to indicate where the fingers should make contact with the pencil.

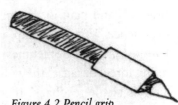

Figure 4.2 Pencil grip

- Use visual and touch cues (e.g. markers) to ensure correct finger placement.

It is important to note that some aids (e.g. pencil grips) encourage the 'normal' grip pattern, which requires more finger strength than the child is able to maintain. In this case they will hamper the child's ability to write, especially if used for extended periods.

The 'normal' grip pattern is called the dynamic tripod grasp. This involves the thumb, index and middle fingers in precise opposition. The wrist is slightly extended, the pencil is grasped near the point and writing movements are made by moving the finger joints, whilst the wrist is held fixed. This posture is usually achieved by 4-and-a-half to 6 years of age. However, the dynamic tripod grasp is not necessarily the best position for all hand shapes and sizes. The gripper will hopefully improve grasp pattern, although dysfunctional grasp patterns are very difficult, or almost impossible, to change as they have become habitual. If it is functional for the child, in that it allows fine movements of the finger joints, an open web space and a stable hand position, then let them carry on using this grasp.

- Use a fibre tip pen.

- Use a pencil with soft lead.

- Use of short crayons/pencils/chalk will encourage the tripod grasp. Whenever the correct grasp is assumed give praise to the child and place paper over a textured surface (template, rough sandpaper, wallpaper) whilst the child scribbles or makes large drawing movements with the crayon, pencil or marker – this helps the child 'get the feel' of the correct finger positioning.

Finger control

If finger movements are awkward, use other activities to develop finger control. Provide regular, supervised practice periods until correct grip position is used automatically – this may take a long time, but plenty of daily practice will eventually pay off.

Normal movement requires normal postural tone (i.e. muscle tension that is neither too high nor too low), so prepare for any desired motor activity by normalising tone as much as possible before presenting activity.

- Stretch a rubber band that is around the fingers by extending the fingers or get the child to stretch bands over the neck of a jar.

- Crumple up stiff paper with one hand, ensuring the child does not do this against his or her chest.

- Pop 'bubble wrap' between finger and thumb.

- Squeeze clothes pegs and move them about a board with nails hammered in it. Perhaps use different coloured pegs to play solitaire, noughts and crosses or draughts.

- Hammer nails into wood, with supervision, or hammer egg trays with a small mallet. Or use a purchased game, e.g. Hammer-Tic/Tap-Tap.

- Use wind-up toys.

In addition, using putty, clay, plasticine or dough will help increase tone before proceeding with written work. Warm-ups like this will particularly benefit 5- or 6-year-olds before starting to write.

Movement in upper limb joints

Poor contol of movement in upper limb joints may be due to poor proprioception and low muscle tone in the joints. This can lead to the child not knowing the position of his or her body parts, not knowing where his or her position in space is and not being able to achieve force control. Poor control of movement is also influenced by inhibition (regulation of movement) and facilitation (speeds up our responses) in our nervous systems if there is not a balance of these elements.

- Use a weighted pen, as this may help slight arm incoordination and reduce tremor and it can provide better joint position.

- Use wrist weights/cuffs. Wrist weights can be purchased in many sport shops or stores like Argos.

- Wrist held down by magnetic cuff on a magnetic board. Magnetic cuffs can be obtained from TfH (see Resources) or can be made by sewing magnetic bars into material and velcroing them to the child's cuff.

Paper moving

This is often due to the child having difficulty coordinating both sides of the body. We use a leading and assistive hand for most bilateral activities, that is, one hand supporting and one hand functional. Persisting reflexes can also affect bilateral coordination, so ensure good sitting posture and give verbal and tactile cues using a stabilising/assistive hand.

- Tape the paper to the tabletop or desk.

- Use a Dycem mat™.

- Use a bulldog clip.

- Use a desk fence. This is a narrow bar of wood round the edges of the tabletop/desk to prevent paper/books from slipping (see Figure 4.3).

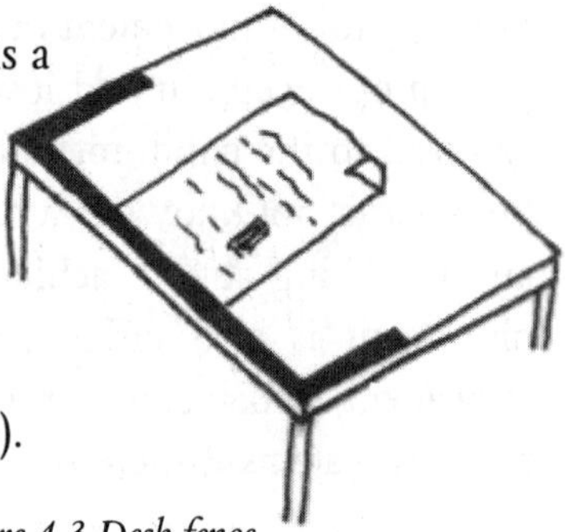

Figure 4.3 Desk fence

Pencil control

Poor pencil control is when a child cannot use a writing implement to form writing patterns that are accurate, fluid and age appropriate. This can be due to the child having physical problems such as poor shoulder stability (so that the whole of the upper limb moves, not just fingers, when writing), low muscle tone in the upper limbs (causing poor force detection), tremor, persisting baby-hood reflexes and poor visual-motor coordination (the inability to coordinate vision with the movements of the body).

- Writing on alternate lines.

- Dots at either side of the page act as markers of where to write from/to, or put left and right hand margins on lined paper.

- The use of wide lined paper may also help as can gridded paper.

- Lined paper turned sideways can help the child to line up numbers.

Final suggestions

- Focus on legibility, rather than neat appearance.

- Allow extra time.

- Use a scribe or Dictaphone™. This helps to focus on the content of a writing assignment and not so much on the placement of letters on lines.

- Stop whenever the child is fatigued. Gradually build up the length of time and amount the child is required to write – too much at one time could cause frustration. Continued laboured writing may require further investigation – if pain, fatigue or very laboured writing occurs word processing may be simpler as there are less fine motor demands. However, remember to minimise visuo-motor aspects of activities whenever possible.

CHAPTER 5

Scissor Skills

Weak hands and fingers are common in children who have difficulty with fine motor skills. These children tend to avoid such activities, but they then do not increase strength in their hands at the rate of children who do engage in fine motor activities at every opportunity. Using scissors can improve many fine motor skills (e.g. bilateral coordination – one hand holding the paper, the other using scissors) and it can increase muscle tone if the child is encouraged to cut through stiff paper or card that provides a bit of resistance. It also encourages motor planning as the child will have to organise the paper and cutting action to change direction. Always tackle simple cutting tasks, such as snipping paper/straws/wool, for, say, a collage, until the child increases their skill, interest and motivation to attempt more intricate cutting out. Ensure the child is using the correct pair of scissors for their dominant hand.

Tips for using scissors

- Use tongs to pick up things – this is a good way to build up strength first.

- Use self-opening scissors or double handled scissors (see Figure 5.1), available from HOPE, GALT and Nottingham Rehab (see Resources), which allow you to control the movement whilst the child can still 'feel' it.

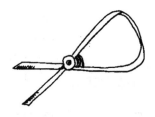

Figure 5.1 Self-opening scissors

- Stick tape or tie yarn around the loops of ordinary scissors so that the blades do not close all the way, or add a rubber band around intersection of blades to keep snips small.

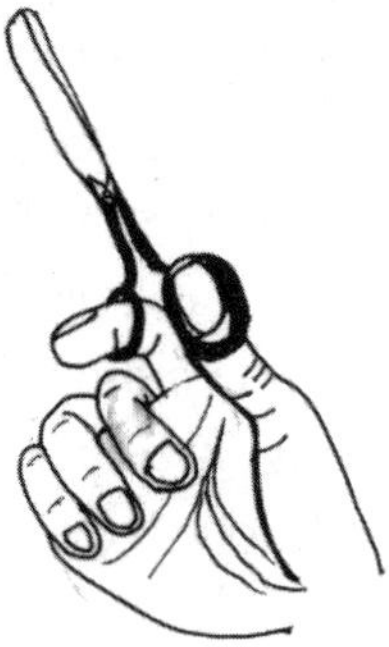

- To use scissors with control, fingers that are not involved in holding the scissors (i.e. the last 2 fingers) are stabilised by touching the palm (see Figure 5.2) Practice open–close hand movements with salad tongs or kitchen tongs.

Figure 5.2 Using scissors – ring and little finger in palm

- Rest the child's forearms on the tabletop if he or she has reduced bilateral coordination (using both hands together). Fatigue sets in if the arms are held up – this provides more stability to the trunk and upper limbs.

- Lie the child on his or her tummy on the floor, resting on his or her forearms and practice

snipping. This position keeps
the trunk, pelvis, shoulders
and elbows still and
aligned, and increases
control in the wrists and
hands.

- Practice snipping and/or
  fringing – straight lines
  are easier. Use cardboard or
  cards or snip straws or
  string into strips.

*Figure 5.3 Reduced bilateral
integration – forearms
resting on table top*

- Practice scissor skills
  regularly and with items of interest that motivate
  the child, such as a scrapbook or collage.

CHAPTER 6

Reading

The DCD child may have reading problems because he or she cannot remember sounds of words or spellings, or because of visual perceptual difficulties (these need to be assessed by a specialist). Often though, the child has problems with poor attention/concentration and with relocation skills (looking quickly from one object to another). If the child loses his or her place due to the former then reading will be difficult and progress will be slow. It is common for children to have difficulty crossing the body midline (an imaginary vertical line down the middle of the body) and this not only affects using the hands when reaching to opposite sides of the body, but the eyes also. The child may read smoothly until the eyes cross the midline and then they 'jump' and lose the place. Moving the eyes quickly from one place to another is also problematic, e.g. looking from a jotter on the desktop to the blackboard and then back to the jotter. This problem with relocation skills can be minimised and remedialised.

Tips for improving reading skills

- Eliminate visual distractions.

- Present small amounts of work at a time.

Figure 6.1 Using an angled surface

- The use of an angled surface to prop the book on, or a book on a stand adjacent or above the paper to avoid losing the place improves eye movements as the child is not having to control lots of different body parts at the same time (see Figure 6.1). Angled surfaces can be obtained from Posturite UK Ltd, Philip & Tacey Ltd and LDA (see Resources).

- Use a 'window' (a narrow rectangle cut out in a piece of card) to isolate sections of text. See Figure 6.2.

- Use a highlighter pen to make relevant/important areas to be read stand out. Some children have problems with figure/ground discrimination (the ability to distinguish an object from its background), so reading text over pictures is difficult.

Figure 6.2 A 'window'

- The teacher or parent can divide syllables by marking with a pencil line throughout the text.

- Use auditory information to supplement visual information. Read material out if necessary, although be sure to check the level of material to be read is suitable.

- Work written on the blackboard should always be sequenced and numbered, so it is easier for the child to follow.

- Use handouts to supplement blackboard work at school.

Under guidance from an Occupational Therapist it is also helpful to provide activities to improve visual perceptual skills and to provide activities to improve eye movements.

Tips for improving visual perceptual skills

Remedial activities for visual perceptual problems vary according to the nature and extent of the difficulties. An OT would use a variety of different activities in fitting with the problem.

- Puzzles

- Sorting games

- Spotting hidden objects in pictures

- Word searches

- Aiming target games

- Matching games

- Dominoes

- Copying pegboard designs

- 'I Spy'

Tips for improving eye movements

Eye movements are important for learning and performing skills such as reading, writing and ball games. If the child has problems with eye movements an OT will suggest activities to encourage the child to exercise the eye muscles.

- Computer games

- Following a marble with the eyes down a marble run (construction game)

- Quickly spotting objects around a room

CHAPTER 7

Feeding

Parents often seek 'normality' when it comes to using cutlery and feeding, but there is always room for compromise. If a child eats with his or her fingers perhaps helping them to use specialised cutlery (see list below) is a preferable alternative. Or cutting up the child's food – giving partial assistance – helps him or her to eat more easily yet still with independence. Such feeding aids can be a great help, but it must be noted that if the child is keen to be the same as his or her peers (e.g. when attending school dinners) such aids might emphasis his or her differences, so perhaps home is where they should be tried out.

Tips for using cutlery and feeding

- Use a Dycem mat™ to stabilise the plate or bowl.

Figure 7.1 Use a Dycem mat™

- The use of a plate guard (a plastic barrier that clips to the edge of the plate, available from Nottingham Rehab – see Resources) or a plate with a lip can also be helpful to prevent food being spilled and can aid a child when he or she is loading up a spoon or fork.

- Moulded cutlery aids finger placement.

- An elastic band around the handles of cutlery helps to prevent the child's fingers from slipping.

- The use of cutlery with built up handles can be helpful if the child's grip is weak. Foam tubing wrapped around the handles works well.

- A splade (see Figure 7.2) can be used if there is a problem with coordinating a knife and fork.

Figure 7.2 A splade

- A sharp steak knife can be used for cutting– but only under supervision!

- Use lightweight cutlery if the child has weakness in his or her upper limbs.

- A lightweight beaker (plastic) is helpful for weakness in upper limbs. This can be bought (see Nottingham Rehab, in Resources) or provided by an occupational therapist.

- Heavy cutlery, weighted cuffs or wrist weights can be helpful if the child has arm tremors.

- A heavy cup (ceramic) can help reduce a tremor or incoordination. This can be bought (see

Nottingham Rehab, in Resources) or provided by an occupational therapist.

- Double-handed cups or cups with anti-spill tops are also useful, as are drinking straws (see Nottingham Rehab in Resources).

- Coordinating a knife and fork can be very difficult for the child and sometimes organisation of the utensils is difficult if there are dyspraxic problems. Get the child to practice cutting Playdoh™ or plasticine regularly. Cutting through material that causes a bit of resistance will also help to increase their muscle tone.

CHAPTER 8

Personal Care
Toileting, Bathing and Grooming

A lot of parents do not like to ask about personal hygiene, but it is a very important and frequent daily task. It is necessary to try and make the child as independent as possible, as they will probably be embarrassed or ashamed to ask for adult assistance when away from home, so for the child's dignity, and to avoid soiling, here are some tips.

Tips for bathing

- If balance is a problem and equipment is required for safely transferring in and out of the bath (e.g. step, bathboard, bath seat, grab bar), then a referral to a community occupational therapist may need to be made (based at your local Social Work Department). You can make a self-referral (or for your child) or you can be referred by your GP, child OT, paediatrician, physiotherapist, speech and language therapist, or, in fact, any professional working with your child.

Tips for toileting

- Ensure the child wears clothing that is easy to pull-off or pull-on, (e.g. minimum of fastenings, elasticated waist, stretchy fabric), so that this lowers the risk of soiling if there is urgency of toileting.

- Cleaning after toileting may be helped if a low mirror is placed adjacent to the toilet, so the child can check his or her personal hygiene.

- Wet wipes may be a help.

- Long-handled wiping aids are available (from Nottingham Rehab – see Resources), but may be more of a hindrance than a help as your child may have problems coordinating and planning its use.

- Often children have bowel and/or bladder problems. If soiling continues after an age you would expect a child to have control, you may need to see an expert, e.g. a Paediatrician, or attend an enuresis clinic. Expert advice should also be sought if your child has constipation.

Tips for grooming

- An electric toothbrush may help when brushing teeth.

- A toothpaste pump dispenser may be easier to use than a tube.

- Long-handled hairbrushes and combs are available if the child cannot reach behind their head, but

organising their use could be problematic if the
child has motor-planning difficulties

- If holding a hairbrush is difficult, use one with a
  strap across it, like a pet's brush.

- Sometimes brushing the opposite side of the head is
  avoided due to poor midline crossing, so encourage
  the child to look in a mirror to check that they
  have completely brushed his or her hair or give a
  verbal prompt to brush the whole of the head.

CHAPTER 9

Dressing

Dressing is a complex activity because there are so many stages involved. To begin with avoid tasks that are difficult unless you or your child really wishes to do the task (e.g. tying shoelaces), as this will only cause frustration and lower the child's confidence. The best way to teach dressing skills is by doing one thing at a time, even if the child begins with only the last stage, e.g. pulling his or her socks up. You can increase the steps involved with each garment gradually, e.g. pull sock over heel and pull up, then tackle putting the sock over the toes, then over the heel and then pull up. By using these 'backward chaining' techniques the child is attaining success, and success leads to increased self-confidence and motivation to try again.

Tips for dressing
Clothing

- Use loose fitting clothes – clothes with elastic waistbands and loose pullovers are ideal.

- Clothes with a minimum of fastenings, such as sweatshirts, T-shirts, jogging trousers or leggings are easier fot the child to manage.

- Stitch a marker to the back of garments to help with orientation.

Buttons, zips and fasteners

- The use of Velcro™ fasteners can make a big difference to any child that has difficulty with ordinary fasteners.

- If the child is fashion conscious you could try stitching buttons on the top of the garment with a Velcro™ fastening below. This will give the garment a 'normal' look so the child should not feel that he or she is wearing anything too different.

- If the child has difficulty with zips, you could try adding a ring to the zip fastener to make it easier to pull the zip up and down (see Figure 9.1).

Figure 9.1 Ring on zip

- Use a button size that is not too small.

- Stitch the top shirt button and the cuff button on with elastic. The top shirt button will have more 'give' to help with fastening and the cuff button can be left fastened and will stretch to allow the hand to go through.

Shoes, socks and ties

- When teaching the child to tie shoelaces, teach just one step at a time until they have mastered that stage. Then go on to teach the next stage and so on.

The use of double twists (repeating the first step of tying a shoelace – putting one lace over and under the other twice before forming a bow) stops the laces coming undone as some children cannot tie laces tightly.

Figure 9.2 Curly laces

- If laces are a problem, use Velcro™ fastening shoes or obtain elastic laces, curly laces (see Figure 9.2) or tags to keep laces fastened. These can be bought (from N G Enterprises – see Resources) or provided by an occupational therapist.

- When choosing socks, choose the tube type as they are easier to manage because they have no heel and should be loose fitting.

- With a tie, using elastic or clip-on fastening can make a difference, or breakdown the task (see tip for shoelaces). Demonstrate how to do up a tie on a teddy or doll first so that the child will be able to see better.

General tips

- If balance is a problem then sit against a wall or in a corner to give stability. This is useful when the child is putting on or pulling off a jacket, when tying shoes or when pulling on tights or trousers – all these things interfere with balance.

- Try listing the order in which clothes are put on, or draw the order on cards (or use pictures or photos) to help show the sequence of putting on clothes.

- Practice daily, using the same set of instructions every time (write down the wording used). A lot of repetition is needed.

- Provide assistance only after the child has made a serious attempt to do the task him- or herself. Encourage him or her to complete dressing tasks independently when there is more time, e.g. at the weekends and during the holidays.

- Remember to give a balance of help and practice so that there is time for other things, e.g. getting to school on time or getting out to play.

- Children with weaker arms may find progress is slower.

Some activities to help

Any activity involving pushing and pulling of arms against some resistance will help strengthen arm muscles (the proprioceptors in the ligaments and joints will be stimulated causing the muscle fibres to tense, hence increasing tone). The activities listed below will increase strength and provide feedback – how movement feels when the body is more stable. However, they will only increase muscle tone and joint stability temporarily so they are worth doing before activities that require fixing the joint in the stabilised position, or fine motor demands. Remember – the more the gross-motor activities are carried out (on a daily basis would be great but if not, 2 to 3 times a week for a short time) the more the child's coordination, postural control and strength will improve.

- Writing or drawing above head height, using whole arm movement.

- Scribbling or colouring over a template is like doing a brass rubbing – the child is applying pressure to create an image on the paper.

- Stirring food, kneading dough and molding putty or clay are entertaining forms of exercise.

- Lifting, pushing, brushing, hoovering and cutting the grass are all good exercise.

- Use a 'Dynaband'™. This is a graded rubber exercise band which can be bought in sports shops (women use them in aerobic classes) or can be obtained from an occupational therapist – they usually provide a 'Theraband'™

Figure 9.3 Using a Dynaband™/Theraband™

which is much the same (see Figure 9.3). These are available from Nottingham Rehab and Smith & Nephew (see Resources).

Figure 9.4 Sitting push ups

- Sitting push-ups or floor push-ups sitting cross legged (see Figure 9.4).

- Wall bars, monkey bars and 'wheelbarrows walking' (walking on hands) all involve sustaining the body weight. As mentioned before this will stretch muscles around the joints and will thereby increase muscle tone and joint stability. In the long term, as these things improve so will coordination.

CHAPTER 10

Attention

There are a number of reasons why children with DCD have problems maintaining attention. First, there could be an overall lack of inhibition in the central nervous system. This makes it hard for the child to regulate or modulate responses. Second, the child may have difficulty with screening, in that he or she finds it hard to filter out the non-relevant and focus on the relevant. This can be visual and/or auditory, e.g. a bird flying past a window or the noise of other children playing outside.

Attention can also be difficult to sustain because the child is putting in far more effort to control his or her body movements than a child who does not have DCD. This means that the child finds it more difficult to stay alert and interested, whilst concentrating on thinking and doing at the same time.

Tips for improving attention

- Reduce sensory distractions in the environment – remove visual distractions, have the work area clean and have the materials close at hand (see Figure 10.1).

Figure 10.1 Minimise eye movements – have reference material close at hand

- Do not use the bedroom for work activities as this is normally associated with sleep, rest and play.

- Adapt activities – break down work periods into smaller segments and increase the attractiveness of the work, e.g. use bright colours.

- Block out non-relevant sensory information – feel movement patterns (i.e. draw/write with eyes closed), block out sounds and use a frame/ 'window' (see Chapter 6) around work, so only the aspect of the work to be done is actually showing.

- Improve communication by seating the child near his or her instructor. Remind the child to focus on the activity, avoid unnecessary words, use clear, specific language, use repetition and check that the child is understanding what is being said.

If the child is lacking in controls (impulsive, heedless, talkative, loud, difficult to manage physically, prone to emotional outbursts and with poor attention) and hyperactive ('on the go' all the time), then other measures may need to be taken.

Tips for improving attention in the hyperactive child

- Wrap the child up in a blanket, duvet, sleeping-bag or gym mat and press your hands firmly down onto him or her and apply sustained pressure for a number of minutes.

- For total body inhibition for calming the child or focusing before fine motor activity, use a blanket to wrap up the child to provide warmth (see Figure 10.2) and maybe use music to help him or her to relax. Providing warmth and slow, repetitive movements by rocking gently back and forth, side-to-side, are all very calming.

Figure 10.2 'Calming' technique

- Cuddling and/or squeezing the child tightly against you, wrapped up, is also effective if deep pressure ('holding') is maintained. This can be done for up to 10 to 15 minutes.

CHAPTER 11

Organisation

Motor-planning difficulty is the inability to plan, organize and execute an unfamiliar task. There are three components to successful motor-planning:

- Forming the idea and knowing what to do.

- Organising the sequence of movement involved in the tasks.

- Carrying out the planned movements in a smooth sequence.

The child with motor-planning problems can have difficulties with one, two or all three of these components. Therefore the child has difficulty figuring out how to use his or her body, and sometimes with organizing his or her behaviour. This can be quite disabling to a child with DCD, causing confusion, severe disorganisation and an illogical method of doing things. It is difficult for many parents and teachers to understand as the child may be very bright yet totally scatterbrained and find it difficult to plan, initiate and execute any activity. Strategies need to be provided to help them with daily activities at home and school, and carers need to have a patient approach.

Tips for organisation

- Give clear, short instructions and give them one step at a time.

- Have consistent, structured routines.

- Keep belongings in a particular place. Make a 'base' so that the child only has to remember and find one place to retrieve books, pencils, paper, gym kit and so on.

- Encourage your child to plan his or her day the night before, e.g. checking that books and items needed for school are in his or her bag.

- Plan your week and stick to activities on the same day and time of week, e.g. swimming on Thursdays at 4.00pm.

- Have a revolving calendar (see Figure 11.1) that the child changes daily, first thing in the morning, so that they know what day and date of the week it is. A watch that displays the day and date, without needing to push a button to get such information, is a good visual reminder of the time and date.

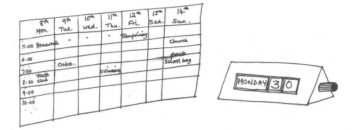

Figure 11.1 Organisers

- Get a person at school to talk through your child's daily routine with him or her at the beginning of each day.

- Encourage your child to always carry a written timetable with him or her to refer to.

- Keep a school diary. Make sure the child writes this up at the end of each class, e.g. what homework has to be done, page references, date for which the homework needs to be completed by and so on.

- Encourage your child to adopt a 'buddy' to assist him or her in getting from class to class, i.e. a consistent friend or auxiliary, especially if your child finds the map of the school difficult to follow or has difficulty with orientation.

- Decide on a mutually agreed award – perhaps for each term – that the child should receive for being independent in managing his or her time, homework and so on. A simple star chart with a realistically achievable score may be a way of measuring success.

- Praise successes and do not emphasise failings or difficulties, so that the child has learned successful behaviour reinforced. (E.g. taking responsibility for organising their own school books/bag is good and if you praise the child – if they are rewarded positively – then they will repeat this behaviour, as they have been successful and been praised for it.)

- Compensate for difficulties by, for example, adapting clothing, using assisting devices, typing instead of writing and avoiding competitive activities and sports.

- Explore other leisure options. Sometimes solitary activities, but within a group without competition, can help improve self-esteem and confidence, e.g. swimming, horse riding, photography, trampolining, using a gym (fixed weights), archery and so on.

- Most importantly, make others (e.g. teachers, peers at school, friends' parents, swimming instructor and so on) aware of the child's problems with organisation so they can provide support and help and do not put too much pressure on the child. They need to create a structured setting for the child also.

CHAPTER 12

Learning New or Difficult Tasks

Learning new tasks will be problematic to the DCD child due to his or her motor and cognitive difficulties. It may be that the child has motor-planning problems, so learning any new task will be difficult. The child will need a lot more practice/repetition of a task and a lot of support, encouragement and patience from the teacher. However, poor attention and concentration can cause the child to have difficulty remembering and sequencing what to do when learning a new task if they cannot stay focused visually or aurally.

It is important to remember that a child with DCD tends to think about movement at a very conscious level, rather than it being automatic. The child is less able to cope with and think about the more sophisticated complex parts of tasks. So if the child is having to think about sitting erect, holding a pencil, listening to the teacher and taking notes all at the same time, then he of she will be putting in much more effort to a task than a child without DCD and he or she will fatigue much quicker.

There are three ways to help a child learn a new or difficult task.

1. Physical help

Place your hand over the child's hand and guide it through the movement. As the child 'feels' the movement and gets the idea, let him or her try more on his or her own. For example, help the child to hold a pencil and draw a circle.

2. Visual clues

Point to what has to be done. For example, point to the spot where the child has to paste the picture or you draw a circle and the child draws a circle by copying what you did.

3. Verbal clues

Tell the child what he or she has to do using clear, simple language. For example:

> 'Draw a big round circle.'

> 'Stick the flower under the tree.'

It is always easier for the child if you use a combination of these cues. Remember that physical help makes it easier for the child, and verbal prompts are more difficult for him or her to interpret. Use the sort of cues that work best for the child.

viour is a Problem

behavioural problems may be primary or secondary to the DCD child. The restlessness, fidgeting and poor performance may be due to a lack of inhibition in the central nervous system, but the child's behaviour may also be a direct result of his or her DCD difficulties. That is, the child may be unhappy, lonely, have poor self-esteem and lack confidence, and he or she develops secondary 'behaviour' problems, such as avoidance, refusal to do things, being withdrawn or acting the clown. The child's behaviour may also be a result of frustration because his or her cognitive ability exceeds his or her achievement.

Reasons for difficult behaviour

Some children may avoid or refuse to do things because they have the following difficulties:

Poor attention

The child has difficulty with screening, i.e. filtering out inappropriate sensory information. The child may be too easily distracted by outside noises, other people or objects in the room, his or her own thoughts and so on. He or she may be fidgety and flit from one activity to another or one place to another.

Poor concentration

The child has difficulty staying focused on a particular task for a reasonable amount of time and is a daydreamer. This may be due to:

- poor attention (easily distracted)

- low muscle tone (tires easily)

- the activity is too difficult

- other activities seem more interesting at the time.

Frustration

The child is easily frustrated. This may be due to:

- poor coordination (clumsiness)

- poor motor-planning (difficulty organising him- or herself)

- poor understanding of language and instructions.

This may result in tantrums, throwing toys, being rough or destructive with toys, or acting in a silly fashion.

Poor self-confidence

The child is so used to struggling or not succeeding, he or she is not really motivated to try. If the child says, "I can't do it!" before really trying, he or she is not being lazy – the child just needs extra encouragement.

What you can do to help at home

Prepare the room to reduce distractions

- Set up an activity in a quiet room in the house.

- Clear the room of as many distracting toys and objects as possible.

- Turn off the television and radio.

- Close the door to shut out other noises.

Also refer to the section on attention (Chapter 10).

Sitting position

- Make sure the child is sitting comfortably.

- Sitting at a table helps keep the child in one place so it is easier for you to keep him or her interested in what he or she is doing.

- There may be times when you want to sit on the floor, but this is difficult with the more active child. Try setting some limits, e.g. 'This special rug is your sitting place. You must sit on the rug if you want me to play with you.'

Also refer to the section on posture (Chapter 3).

Give clear, simple instructions

- Keep your language simple.

- Give one simple step at a time to start with, e.g. 'First, Jimmy, sit down.' (Help him to sit) 'Where are Jimmy's pencils?'

- Help the child to direct himself by asking him simple questions or requests, e.g. 'What colour pencil next?'; 'Where will you paste the first flower?'

Also refer to the section on organization (Chapter 11).

Redirection

- Help the child to stay with the activity by redirecting him physically, visually and/or verbally back to what he was doing.

- Observe when the child has had enough of the activity or has become too tired.

- Help the child to finish the activity within a reasonable amount of time, so he or she will be interested in trying again on another occasion.

- If necessary, gain perseverance of an activity by describing the next event, e.g. 'Come and sit down…then we can have a new toy.'

Completing tasks

- Use turn-taking. This helps speed up the activity, encourages active participation and is important for communication and interaction, e.g. 'I'll stick on the red flower…which one will you do?'

- Indicate when the activity is finished. If the child indicates he doesn't want the toy or activity any more, help him to put the toy away or to tidy up.

- Use turn-taking, e.g. 'You do the blue ones, I'll do the green ones.'

- Praise the child for helping as this will make him or her feel good and want to cooperate again next time.

Setting limits and expectations

- If cooperation and/or attention is a problem, it may help to set some simple boundaries for the child, e.g. 'If you want to play you must sit down first.'; 'One more bead to thread, then we will finish.'; 'Which one will you do – yellow or blue?'

- Giving the child a simple choice can help cooperation.

- Give praise for cooperation and staying within the set limits, e.g. 'Good sitting. What do you want to do next – threading or the puzzle?'

Praising and encouragement

This is really important for developing the child's self-confidence. If the child feels good about doing something, he or she will hopefully want to do it again.

- Verbal praise, smiles or rewards can be used, e.g. stickers or special toys or activities. The latter is often best when behaviour is more difficult.

- Do not wait until the activity is complete before praising – give encouragement for each small part the child does, e.g. 'Good try! You did it!'

- Give the child the opportunity to try things his way rather than always the way you would do the task. This helps the child to develop an inner sense of achievement.

Individual versus group

- When motivation is a problem the child might be happier to do a task with friends or other family members.

- The child may be motivated more by social reasons than by the task itself.

- You will often find the child will do things for others but not with you at home.

CHAPTER 14

Activity Suggestions for Developing Motor Skills

Children with DCD often feel floppy around joints and tire quickly with physical activity as a result of poor tone and joint stability. Any activity that provides pressure that is greater than the weight of the body part into a joint (joint compression) will stimulate the muscles around the joint and increase stability at that joint, and thus will increase muscle tone.

The choice of activity depends on the problem, so get guidance from your occupational therapist. Nevertheless, there are some general activities you could use to develop physical skills, and the following suggestions could be carried out with individuals or a group of children with similar difficulties. For the child's safety, always supervise the child when carrying out activities, checking for correct positioning and providing assistance if required. Make sure the child works on a padded mat or gym mat.

The activities listed can be used by parents, by teachers or by carers of children with DCD and can be adapted for home or classroom use. The activities should be fun and feel good to the child and the aim is to focus attention on the outcome, not the action required to fulfil it. For example, the object of a game is to catch a ball above the head, not to think about the reaction and extending the arms.

You should try, if at all possible, not to instruct the child on how to perform with various body parts. Self-direction is the key. Children learn most when they 'feel' the body position and do this for themselves.

Do not insist that the child does the activity if the child expresses extreme dislike or disinterest. Avoid the activity and do something else. Cooperation is changeable and they may be willing to try another day. If the child is tiring with a task stop it and go on to another activity.

Try to do the activities regularly, daily or at least 3 to 4 times a week, with more short periods being better than one long period. Work at roughly the same time of the day – mornings are probably best because the child is not so fatigued. Remember to praise and encourage all efforts and achievements.

Proprioceptive activities

When carrying out a therapeutic programme for the child, first use activities providing proprioceptive input (those that provide information about the state and condition of the muscles, tendons and joints). Then follow it with an activity that will use the joint in the stabilised position.

Activities providing proprioceptive input

- Tug-of-war.

- Swinging from gym bars.

- Climbing on playground equipment.

- Punchball/bag or 'boxing' into a pillow.

- Play fighting: push/pull the child by his or her hands and try and make the child work really hard and not fall over.

- Trampolining: on feet, in high-kneeling position or on an old mattress on floor.

- Jumping on a space hopper (see Figure 14.1).

- Push feet against a wall, a large beanbag or with a partner.

- 'Push-offs' from a wall with hands, from bent elbows to straight arms.

Figure 14.1 A space hopper

- Being pushed on a scooterboard (a flat, rectangular board with rounded edges and four castor wheels beneath – available from TfH and Rompa, see Resources): lay the child in prone (on tummy) with arms and legs extended, then push him or her by the ankles and let him or her crash into stacked cardboard boxes/soft play blocks/skittles (see Figure 14.2).

Figure 14.2 Prone position on a scooterboard

- Building with tools and construction kits.

- Any hammering, e.g. large egg trays – hammering 'bumps'.

- Stapling papers or using a hole punch.

Activities that use the joint in a stabilised position

- Supporting self on forearms in prone when playing a game, e.g. throwing beanbags at targets.

- Suspend an object from a rope and get the child to lie in front or to side in prone and attempt to bat it from this position.

  - Grab a rope suspended above when lying in prone and pull up as far as possible – the aim is to get to a standing position (see Figure 14.3).

  - Crawling activities, e.g. 'commando', on hands and knees, obstacle courses and relays.

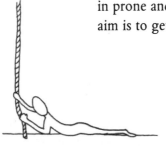

Figure 14.3 Pulling self up from prone

- Side-sitting (see Figure 14.4) to read or play a game to twist the trunk, e.g. knocking down skittles in an arc.

- Use a scooterboard. Self-propel in prone around obstacles or in relays.

Figure 14.4 Side-sitting

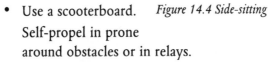

- Wheelbarrow walking.

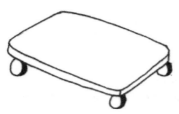

Figure 14.5 A scooterboard. This can be covered in carpet for tactile stim-ulation , and a play barrel can be lined with carpet also.

Always check that the child's joints are aligned correctly, with no hyperextension of wrists or elbows.

Vestibular activites

Activities providing other sensory stimulation are also required to improve motor skills, such as. vestibular activities (the orientation of the body in space as it changes position). Carry these out next.

Rolling activities

- On mats, roll from one end to the other and back. A variation on this is to roll over scattered beanbags and other uneven surfaces.

- A resisted roll. Hold the child at his or her hips, which means that the child's upper trunk must rotate before turning over.

- Rolling in a play barrel (suppliers are Rompa, Nes Arnold, GALT and TfH – see Resources), with the head and neck outside, and roll down a mat and back. A variation on this is to roll over soft skittles or cones to knock them down, or roll to different parts of room. See Figure 14.6.

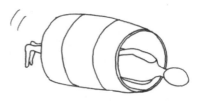

Figure 14.6 Rolling in a play barrel

Balance activities

- Balance beam. Walk the length of the beam, forward, backwards and sideways (use a wide beam initially then, as child improves, use narrow beam).

- Rocker board. Balance or rock in standing, sitting and kneeling positions and engage in various games, such as catching/throwing beanbags, batting a balloon, tossing quoits over pegs or playing a magnetic fishing game with a rod, whilst rocking back and forth.

- T-stools. Sit on the stools, performing various games, such as throwing and catching balls or beanbags or kicking them at targets. T-stools need to be made by a handyman, technical instructor or sheltered workshop.

Figure 14.7 A T-stool
(approximate size- 26cm (L) x
13 cm (W) x 17cm (H))

Rapid change activities

- Swinging. Sit and/or hang onto a large rope in a gym, swing back and forth and pick up objects from floor whilst swinging.

- 'Hot dog'. Roll up the child in a blanket then pull it quickly so that he or she rolls out.

- 'Parachute'. A child lies down or sits on a 'parachute' in the centre of a group. The group walks around, wrapping up the child, then everyone pulls the parachute back, causing the child to be swung around and released (available from GALT, Nes Arnold and Rompa – see Resources).

- Trampolining. Try simple jumping, knee drops, seat drops, quarter turns whilst standing (to the right and left), half turns whilst standing (to the right and left) and a full turn if possible. For motor-planning, jump and swing arms in circles and in the reverse direction. Try one arm forward and one back when jumping or 'swimming' with the arms whilst jumping.

Tactile activities

Also carry out tactile activities (for distinguishing the self from the outside environment) to provide further sensory stimulation. These are also required to improve motor skills.

- Hand lotion. The child rubs lotion onto arms, hands, legs – whatever skin is available.

- Shaving foam. The child rubs foam over arms, hands and legs and then get him or her to scrape off the foam firmly, using a spatula or cloth.

- 'Feely box'. Put either polystyrene chips, shredded paper, rice, lentils, pasta or sand in a box. Hide objects within these materials and then the child feels for the hidden objects. If the box is big enough the child could climb inside – wear shorts and a T-shirt for maximum sensory input.

- Textured cloths (foam, carpet, fur, wool, sandpaper, wallpaper, velvet, bubblewrap and so on). Blindfold the child and get him or her to identify which item is being rubbed over his or her skin surface.

- Blind walk. Lead the blind-folded child around the room and present as many objects as possible for him or her to identify.

- Imaginary painting. Pretend to paint body parts with a large brush, applying deep pressure and wipe off specific colours with different textured materials.

- 'Hamburger'. The child lies on one blanket/mat/duvet whilst you add textures for 'relish', 'lettuce' and so on, then cover with another blanket/mat/duvet and push down on the child with your hands or an inflatable roll or bolster.

- 'Swiss roll'. The child rolls up in bubblewrap/corrugated card/blanket/rug and then unrolls him- or herself.

- 'Caterpillar'. The child goes into a sleeping bag and then crawls, rolls, wriggles, curls up and elongates to make a movement like a caterpillar.

- 'Snail'. The child 'commando crawls' with a large beanbag on his or her back, crawling under and around things and curling into shell.

Figure 14.8 The 'snail'

- 'Tank'. Join together the ends of a large piece of corrugated card to form loop. The child climbs inside and crawls or steps to make it move.

- 'Parachute'. In a circle, one child stands or lies in the centre of a 'parachute'. The group lifts their arms up and down to make the parachute billow and lightly touch child in the centre. The group lifts the parachute, and as it billows up one or more children run under and quickly lie down waiting for the parachute to descend on them.

Planned movement, hand–eye coordination and orientation in space activities

Follow the proprioceptive, vestibular and tactile activities with ones that require planned movement, hand–eye coordination and orientation in space. The following activities are good for improving these skills.

- Imitating postures using arms, legs, hands and fingers. Play 'Simon Says'.

- Animal walks, e.g. bunnyhops, crab walk, bear walk, wiggly worm, caterpillar or donkey.

- Twister™ game (see Figure 14.9).

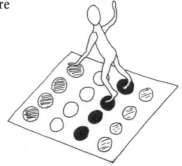

- Obstacle courses using chairs, table, bed, blankets – whatever is available for the child to go over, under, through, around, behind and so on.

Figure 14.9 Twister™

- Sequencing movements, e.g. first skip, then jump, then crawl around a simple obstacle course.

- Beanbag throwing across the body into a box or at a target.

- Beanbag games, e.g. between legs, behind back, overhead and so on. Play 'Hot Potato' (passing the beanbag around in a circle as fast as possible and then reverse unexpectedly).

- Ball games. Initially catch the ball by holding a box to catch it in, then use hands. Try throwing against a wall, catch bouncing on floor, dribbling around objects by bouncing or using feet, throwing against a wall to hit the centre of a coloured shape (circle, triangle, square, diamond, hexagon) or knocking down targets (e.g. bowling).

- Ball pass. In a circle, pass various sized, textured and weighted balls around and change direction.

- Dodge ball.

- Balloons. In a circle, hit the balloon with a bat or hand and try to keep it up in the air and prevent it from hitting the ground – volleyball with a balloon.

- Stepping stones, using carpet squares. The child can walk on all fours, leap, jump and so on from square to square. Encourage sequencing by using different coloured squares for different movements.

- Rope jumps. Lay a rope on floor in an irregular way, crossing the rope over itself. The child has to walk along the rope and jump with his or her feet together over the crossed areas.

- Rope walk. Step sideways along rope, crossing one foot over the other.

- Jumping. Two people hold a rope and one-by-one the group jumps over the rope as it 'snakes' on the ground. Do not land on the slithering snake! Then jump over a taut rope and gradually increase height with each jump.

- Skipping.

- Walking/running games, e.g. backwards, forwards, sideways, big steps, small, high, low, crawl, in all directions, like a crab, fast, slow, 'freeze' to hold position and so on.

Figure 14.10 Pushing

- Pulling/pushing. In pairs, hold hands tightly and each child leans back and tries to pull the other one out of their starting spot. Then try in pairs, back to back, as above (see Figure 14.10). This can be done in a sitting position as well.

- Mirroring. In pairs one person will move, whilst the other imagines he is a mirror. The mirror follows his partner as accurately as possible. Switch roles.

- Ball batting. Stand behind the child and pitch a ball. The child holding the bat must swing around in order to hit the ball.

The end of the session

End your session with a calming down activity. Relaxation is one option: have the child lie on his or her back, concentrating on different body parts (to develop better awareness of their positions) and pushing them into the floor from head to toes. Another option is to get the child to work at a tabletop activity (see list below) that requires concentration, visual attention, visual discrimination, organisational skills and hand–eye coordination.

- Build a Lego® model, copying the diagram.

- Maze board/tray or 'Labyrinth Game' (available from toy retailers, TfH and Rompa – see Resources).

- Puzzles.

- Board games – following rules and/or involving memory.

Activities for finger and hand strength

Do not forget to give the child lots of opportunity to increase finger and hand strength also, with a variety of day-to-day activities:

- wringing out cloths

- using clothes pegs

- tongs/tweezers

- hammering

- tiddlywinks

- wind-up toys

- pop beads (interlocking plastic beads)

- nuts and bolts

- crumpling paper (stiff paper) – use fingers, not against chest

- stapling/punching paper

- clay/plasticine/wet sand – get the child to draw lines using a stick or pointed forefinger, then use as a pencil.

All these activities are only suggestions – please let the child use his or her imagination when engaged in tasks. If you can think of any other activities along the same lines please use them. I hope these ideas will give all parents and carers of children with DCD a head start in implementing a therapeutic programme, especially teachers who may wish to start a group at school.

Final Note

As a final note, please remember to bear in mind the key points mentioned in the Introduction and remember that the children need sympathy and understanding.

- **Allow extra time**
- **Do lots of practice**
- **Praise successes**
- **Use repetition**
- **Do not pressure**
- **Allow variability**

A child's performance will be variable from day-to-day, even from hour-to-hour. **Please remember this!**

Helpful Addresses

AFASIC
69–85 Old Street
London
EC4 9HX

Tel: 020 7841 8900

British Dyslexia Association
98 London Road
Reading
RG1 5AU

Tel: 0118 966 8271/2

Children in the Highlands Information Point (CHIP)
Birnie Child Development Centre
Raigmore Hospital Grounds
Inverness
IV1 3UJ

Tel: 01463 711 189

Contact A Family (CAF)
209–211 City Road
London
EC4 1JN

Tel: 020 7608 8700

Contact a Family (CAF) Scotland
Norton Park
57 Albion Road
Edinburgh
EH7 5QY

Tel: 0131 475 2608

Dyspraxia Foundation
8 West Alley
Hitchin
Herts
SG5 1EG

Tel: 01462 454 986

ENQUIRE (Independent Advice on Special Educational Needs)
Children in Scotland
Princes House
5 Shandwick Place
Edinburgh
EH2 4RG

Tel: 0131 222 2424

Independent Special Educational Advice (ISEA)
164 High Street
Dalkeith
LH22 1AY

Tel: 0131 454 0096

National Association for Paediatric Occupational Therapists
65 Prestbury Road

Wilmslow
Cheshire
SK9 2LL

Tel: 01625 549 266
Fax: 01625 530 680

National Autistic Society
393 City Road
London
EC4 1NG

Tel: 020 7833 2299

**Scottish Dyslexia
Association**
Stirling Business Centre
Wellgreen
Stirling
F88 9D2

Tel: 01786 446 650

**Scottish Society for Autistic
Children**
Hilton House
Alloa Business Park
Whins Road
Alloa
FK10 3SA

Tel: 01259 720 044

**Scottish Support for
Learning Association (SSLA)**
Bill Sadler
4 Woodside Avenue
Grantown-on-Spey
PH26 3JN

Tel: 01479 872 480

Resources

GALT
Culvert Street
Oldham
Lancashire
OL4 2GE

Tel: 0161 627 5086

E-mail:
orders@galt-educational.co.uk

G & S Smirthwaite Ltd
16 Wentworth Road
Heathfield
Newton Abbot
Devon
TQ12 6TL

HOPE EDUCATION
Orb Mill
Huddersfield Road
Watehead
Oldham
Lancashire
OL4 2ST

LDA
Duke Street
Wisbech
Cambridgeshire
PE13 2AE

NES ARNOLD Ltd
Ludlow Hill Road
West Bridgeford
Nottingham
NG2 6HD

Tel: 0115 971 7700

NG Enterprises
4 Swan Mead
Ringwood
Hants
BH24 3RD

Nottingham Rehab Supplies
A Division of Novara Group Ltd
Novara House
Excelsior Road
Ashby de la Zouch
Leicestershire
LE65 1NG

Tel: 0870 6000 197

E-mail: www.nrs-uk.co.uk

Philip & Tacey Ltd
North Way
Andover
Hants
SP10 5BA

Posturite UK Ltd
P.O. Box 468
Hailsham
East Sussex
BN27 4LZ

Rifton Equipment
Robertsbridge
East Sussex
TN32 5DR

Rompa
Goyt Side Road
Chesterfield
Derbyshire
S40 2PH

Tel: 0800 056 2323

E-mail: sales@rompa.com

www.rompa.com

Smith & Nephew
Homecraft Ltd.
P.O.Box 5665
Kirby-in-Ashfield
Notts
NG17 7QX

Tfh
5-7 Severnside Business Park
Stourport-on-Severn
DY13 9HT

Tel: 01299 827 820

E-mail: tfh@tfhuk.com

www.tfhuk.com

Bibliography

Ayres, A.J. (1987) *Sensory Integration and the Child.* Los Angeles: Western Psychological Services.

Dyspraxia Foundation (1998) *Recognising Developmental Coordination Disorders: Developmental Dyspraxia Explained.* Hitchin, UK: Dyspraxia Foundation.

Fink, B.E. (1989) *Sensory-Motor Integration Activities.* Arizona: Therapy Skills Builders; a Division of the Psychological Corporation.

Levine, K.J. (1991) *Fine Motor Dysfunction: Therapeutic Strategies in the Classroom.* Arizona: Therapy Skill Builders; a Division of the Psychological Corporation.

Stephenson, E., in association with The Scottish Occupational Therapy DCD Clinical Network (2000) *The Child with Developmental Coordination Disorder (Motor/Learning Difficulties including Dyspraxia): A Guide for Parents and Teachers.* Aberdeen: Waverly Press.

Index

active participation 64
activities of daily living (ADLs) 10, 17
activity suggestions for developing motor skills 67–79
    activities for finger and hand strength 79
    end of session 78
    planned movement, hand–eye coordination and orientation in space activities 75–8
    proprioceptive activities 68–71
    vestibular activities 71–5
aerobics 49
AFASIC 83
angled surface 19, 34
animal walks 75
archery 58
arm(s)
    movements 19
    strengthening muscles 48
armrests, chair 18
Asperger Sydrome (AS) 9
assistance, rationing of 48
attention
    problems 33, 51–3, 59, 61–2, 65
    span, reduced 17
    tips for improving 51–3
    tips for improving attention in hyperactive child 53
Attention Deficit Hyperactivity Disorder (ADHD) 9
    tips for improving attention in hyperactive child 53
auxiliaries 57
avoidance 61
award system 57
Ayres, A.J. 87

baby-hood reflexes, persisting 17, 19, 21, 26
backward chaining techniques 45
balance
    activities 72
    beam 72

    problems 14, 41, 47
Ball, R. 7
ball
    batting 78
    dodge 76
    games 76
    pass 76
balloon, batting 72, 77
bath 41
bathboard 41
bathing, tips for 41
bath seat 41
beanbags 69, 70, 71
    games 76
    throwing/catching 72, 76
bear walk 75
bedroom 52
behavioural problems 13, 15, 61–6
    reasons for difficult behaviour 61–2
        frustration 62
        poor attention 61–2
        poor concentration 62
        poor self-confidence 62
    what you can do to help at home 63–6
        completing tasks 64–5
        give clear, simple instructions 63–4
        individual versus group 66
        praising and encouragement 65–6
        prepare room to reduce distractions 63
        redirection 64
        setting limits and expectations 65
        sitting position 63
belongings, keep in particular place 56
bilateral coordination 25, 29, 30, 31
blanket, wrapping child in 53, 73
blind walk 74
board games 78
body inhibition for calming or focusing child 53
body midline crossing 33
boundaries, setting 65
bowel/bladder problems 42
'boxing' into pillow 68